—SplitLevel Texts

PRACTICE

SplitLevel Texts
Ann Arbor, MI 48103
http://www.splitleveltexts.com

Cover Image "Muqarnas," pigment print, 2005, by Brent Wahl

ISBN: 978-0-9858111-6-7

Library of Congress Control Number: 2015932224

PRACTICE

Laynie Browne

for my grandmother
Lillian Browne 1912-2014
in loving memory

You cannot fold a Flood—
And put it in a Drawer—
Because the Winds would find it out—
And tell your Cedar Floor—

—Emily Dickinson

"Where else would you start to drown and suddenly be in a new body?
Where else would you see the meagerness of your own expression as
a corpse? Where else might you be a torso, beating at your own
window?"

—Alice Notley

"Kierkegaard says knowledge proceeds every act but surely there
are acts that are not proceeded by knowledge. Repetitions pass at the
front door from summer to winter. Some slowly. Some quickly. Total
strangers. Never saw them before. Can't picture them now. Umbrellas—
strange totalities—upheld, wheeling."

—Lyn Hejinian

"Does absence occupy time, is absence a new moment? Does it have its
own sort of presence?"

—Norman Fischer

"They threaten to throw into the air their own aura that becomes a
ghost."

—Clarice Lispector

1.

Practice replacing one thought with another. Rough heel replaces soft consciousness. 10:35 am replaces 9:35 am. Where our bodies reside in space is not probable. Replace this emptiness with a quotation: "Temptations thronging through my hours are strong." Replace sugar with sweetness. I said, I don't know how to be helpful to you now, and he said, replace bitterness with turnstiles, complacency with walking. When that voice appears that claims we must all be dead, replace non-wakeful living with the milk of a dark blue star you keep with the pudding string. Do not replace childhood, but when it replaces itself in your children practice going to the well. If you lay down on the ground, rise up again.

2.

Do not allow any single book to take over. Practice does not make a nineteenth-century folk-song which has long been worn for whittles. As your hand moves to click a virtual scene practice withdrawing iron pots and ebony. Wearing a face you wish to inhabit. So you want to make glass from just waiting? Practice what you fear. This needs no practice. Replace siphons with wares, and what is knotted with breath.

3.

Practice not keeping anything. When a child is threshed and winnowed, when quietus claims a windlass, practice wishing you could be someone who knows how to place a net or face in front of the oxlips. How to speak underwater, how to form grooved strips of lead into sounds, and how enter a palm of interlaced days gladly.

4.

Practice writing something which does not fall into didacticism or seek to emulate but is informed by untarnished black ribbing, bannisters, railway stations. You want the grease on your hands. You wish to ruin your clothes if this may be necessary. Replace appetites for singular pleasure with appetites for lending. You don't mind coal smudges on your fingers but you do care that they do not intrude further.

5.

Practice remembering any interior. This requires that you record your misfortunes here, in no uncertain terms. Am I allowed to check? I've distrusted my hands so many times, in multiple registers. Do I pardon my own roving abandonment? Speak as if you know nothing. Collect yourself in a rain barrel. Read yourself into a place you'd like to be.

6.

Practice stepping inside an increment of time that has not yet been described. Bring only your arms and your thoughts. Do not allow yourself to sleep, correspond or complain. Mark this time solely for what might happen. Attach yourself to this increment and refuse to allow your arms or your thoughts to depart. Your only container is a clock. Practice remaining in time with yourself. Fix a similar increment in your memory so that you may repeat this wading tomorrow.

7.

Practice promising something. Go to the nearest bridge. You will be accompanied by harp and bicycle. Practice falling. Then replace falling with waterborne-thought. Is it really as easy as deciding to bow your head, to remember warriors undaunted, even as they plummet? Is anything as deceptively simple as breath? What makes an increment? What makes a bridge? Practice replacing accompaniment with whatever sounds surround you. Dress yourself in beasts and rain-glossed verbs.

8.

When one cannot say where one has been a silver light overhangs violin cliffs. A running pack comes into relief. Practice running with the overhang or changing location often. You are not carnivorous and you are not part of the pack. Practice running short of breath and imagine silver where there are only false mountains. Practice looking up into pleats of light as if they could divine your thoughts.

9.

Practice noting yourself within a body, a location as real or unreal as violin cliffs, stark overhangings of doubt, the barren cavity of a hunting animal. I practiced this sentence repeatedly after her passing: Why am I still in body? Your thoughts may be changing location as often as gold and pink bones. Practice imagining you wear an exoskeleton. Things are easier when you lope across pretend distances you cannot fathom. Practice memorizing summer, where your torn and transparent aspect cannot be disregarded, but is repeatedly shorn.

10.

I practiced repeating the sentence: I cannot say who anyone will become, what misgivings accompany the pleated waking of the unreal, or why some of us remain. Do I dare to descend the stairs?

11.

Practice leaving home continuously. Practice where you have been. What it will sound like. When you are absent. No flutter. Bend knees. Silence return.

Practice not asking questions when you hear the cello aligned with itself repeatedly. Practice symphonic unknowing—believing you inhabit a summons. Look away from yourself. Memorize cloud sets. The movement of lips. Whose lips?

Once I practiced a vote to uphold your weather. Once you practiced maintaining a pillar of unearthly sounds. Once rebels practiced a farewell parachute. But that was once, or not at all.

12.

Practice alphabets with your body. Stop reading blinkers. These are not commands—I barely remember.

Replace fire with bronze ingots, a bright stage. Energy multiplied by mass reveals lament. Who is coming to see us? Shall we linger on the unspeakable? How have we succumbed without knowing the name of another's loss?

If you walk into water up to your waist you understand weightedness but also transparency. You read inscriptions on your skin, yet still expect to rouse.

13.

If you find yourself rummaging through vacant fields which you once deemed pregnant, sit with reservations. I've packed the animal spirit cards. Which way now? How to douse? Our conversation will be without missives. Practice complaining less than two minutes each day. Practice a delicate hand of—.

14.

Practice in the rain under a porch on a second story. What is like this quiet? Practice serpentine—a very loud bird. A far away voice. As they pull away it stops raining. Practice anyone else's life. Moments when hands are flimsy, almost beyond gesture. Leanings, in a river searching for salamanders, new ways you may be culled.

15.

Practice the date born wet and unctuous

Practice words or walking

You've never not been

Irrecoverable wish

Cabbage white butterfly

Nascent quiver

Against your will

16.

Where are you, embodied?

I searched for a correct candle

Don't bother to burrow, dress or haul

I'll write this again later, over and under the foliage

Practice a park within a furnace

Abandonment could be so lovely with fern-like paths—but it is not

17.

Woodpile shivers water. I am older than I've ever been, even before yesterday. Is it the branches above or is it the evening before, remembered by overhanging pine? Practice saying nothing about the apparition. Naming the droplets: how to be compact; a chair at the head of one's bed, a boy hung back, the other side of the pane.

18.

Practice repeating: *their trucks are fully stocked*

Stranded, would be best

Or tacit description of—

How to answer again

Melt countertops

I'm going to help you up this flight

Pasty, train whistle, dialogue

Do I dare descend the stares?

Practice what you probably—don't know

19.

Practice existing through cloistered fire, as if you had been written before, in a form-fitting century, distinct from others you might have inhabited in thought only. Pulling duckweed from faces—you swim through inevitable chandelier boughs.

20.

Walk by woodpile shadowed by boy walking with stick, his face a compression of clouds. Felled limbs become shadow, lifting birch hatchet. His arm swings. Are you ready as something leaps, some anatomy you cannot name, sharp enough to startle? Practice response with no language. Determining your whereabouts. How long have you slumbered?

21.

When you walk upstairs, listen to the wood. Practice standing in plain sight where no one can see you.

We found the missing stone water tower, at the edge of the garden. All but one other have vanished. What appears to be a moat is close to nothing.

At a table earlier in the day, where words may gather, phosphorescently, upon your fingertips, practice what they unsay to you, as if you did not speak this particular language.

22.

I do not imply deaf utterance, arch denials or henna applied to tongue.

Practice speaking to each thud as it is unpacked, placed upon a cartwheel.

Forgetting the difference between verbs and nouns, possessive and personal. Practice standing at the border of a piano, where you wait to enter a demonstration utterance.

Practice saying nothing as you stand there, not making eye contact with anyone, thinking thoughts only you will know.

23.

Practice inhabiting at least one hour when you are entirely awake. This may require you to disregard a console, missile or insurgent reaching for your arm or texts spread in front of you as so much wreckage.

Replace thoughts of travel with legalization of resident wind, caustic light, postal smudging.

Replace doubt in your ability to be still with the empty space that inhabits a stair. When you step, place not only your foot—but also the arched intent to float, gravity dropped. Ferns frame your perspective.

24.

If you find yourself still hearing a particular voice which intrudes upon your water tower, practice dismissing the voice through the following means:

1. The voice can only exist within possessive constructs
2. You are not inside a sleeping noun
3. The voice depends entirely upon your courtesy

25.

Practice looking far up the trunk of an incarnate spectacle

Remembering your name, as you would wish anyone else to recall an arboreal chandelier, a variant of Helen.

Practice listing the names of those you trust. Cover their faces with filigreed air, divulged utterance. Tell them—your mouth preserved with lime.

Walk back remembering verdancy

Practice not obliging a gleaming custom which does not match your future.

26.

When you have no words and someone mocks you from inside a brook, practice you are sibling to that water.

You are not a looking glass of disgruntled children. When you lovingly push the curls from their eyes practice reciting the same good fortune into their ears, silently, as if you had maps to the thoughts they will not disclose.

Who are you, isn't at all, or may be, your only balm.

27.

Practice writing letters of recommendation for various species you hope will continue

Wolves, devour description, hunt

Prairie dogs, poisoned by social order, dig

Black bear, powers and duties, retreat to the woods

28.

Yes it is getting to that, that I cannot look back. There are no tracks behind me, and none ahead.

I have almost

Stopped checking whereabouts

Stop—

Is anything retrievable?

29.

Courting an absence—to what end I cannot say

Liminal space is soon to be replaced

Do not forget oblivion

The lost apparatus, holding nothing in one's hands

No one believed I meant to compliment their wolves

I had forgotten this space of intent

But they aren't wolves, the strangers insisted

We never wanted to leave the shore

I wish my eyes were not tired and your thoughts

Did not retreat to a far corner I cannot hear

When one is cornered possibility expands

How grateful I have become to such a short time

30.

Practice introducing yourself through silence. Walk to a meeting house. The room is warm. Nudge certain cats and a small coffin-like fiddle case away.

Draughts complete with blooming miles. Practice lostness without bothering about ashes or extinguished moons.

Greet each spine with remembering. Pause to sit on the floor and turn pages.

Practice slowing until alphabetical arrangements become secondary to the smallest threshold you can read.

31.

And go sometimes with no memory of draughts. You are sitting beside
your beloved. How hard will you try? If you miss the turn twice do
you try a third time? I am attempting to enter the realm where I refuse
to talk silver-headed. So he'll take a longer time to instruct his valve
usage, his posture and embouchure. How does one spell a lane which
unfolds? I don't dare ask or break a small stitch of silence. She said:
this is how I picture you, where one highway bleeds to another.

32.

Don't practice loss, though when it arises chant through the
sauntering chasms. There is one photograph I imagine as penultimate,
although none of us are still living. Is it weakness to fall into lament as
suddenly as the lilt of a voice? There are others I dare not play. And
how did I make it past the first year of absence? One sharp exhale,
fallen to the ground. What spell is this? It has inhabited me the way
I might embody a likeness to a figure in a painting, the way a wood
encompasses sight. The way a gown enfolds a body inside this dearth
where the softest shadow chafes.

33.

A heavy countenance draws curtains across your brow. See even where there is none to see at all. Practice when you are bidden, coming to account for lost beads of water about your throat, stolen topaz. Who you were once in a photograph cannot be relied upon. Recall the encircling, now hidden. Looking out a picture window the landscape is dotted with squirrels turned rigid bronze. The gaze which looks out at you may never have happened as you remember it.

34.

You are a rook seen through a poison glass

Asked to unburden yourself from what you call 'certainty'

Pulled taut an ember spilt from forgiving fingers

A(verse) which cannot be dislodged from memory

Your face will not tarnish

Sewn through copper estuaries

What others exhale does not afford your wake

Do I dare descend the stars?

35.

Do not wade out, but imagine the dropped beads of water existing somewhere.

You are not tossed as a blanket, woven of crooked stares, divided as a morning darkens, bifurcated as abstraction covets, a rook seen through a poison glass.

36.

Practice time as a rivulet you might mention persuasively as dusk passes. The wave escorts your carriage darkening nothing. Stillness requires flame, apothecaries hewn from fallen limbs. Practice waking before the onslaught to gather a name which comforts ash. You know how to form the words between extinguish and incarnate.

37.

Practice who you are called to become when inseams gather your lip. One moment you are speaking with fluid ease. Cakes of soap press.

A rifle is mentioned—and a coat—as a fox crosses your path. Your existence is based entirely upon the warmth of the animal running away from you.

38.

Where would you go, unleashed from supposition? In smallness of features is examination of one's own tattered pockets. Suppose you were to pull a face closer instead of staring into distances. Suppose the game were broke and gesture meant nothing. Would you reveal a door of your own making—and shove?

39.

Practice the version of yourself you must pardon, the one with fragile lips, drifting into late. Beyond doors, where would you go, unleashed? I searched for the blossom with which to paint the expression for retrieval of cordials. Where loneliness is as vast as unbecoming I could not find the balm. I went out in several frocks, coats, and dresses only to realize that I had left my fingers at home. And all of my necessary sources of red.

40.

Practice daring symptoms to disperse

A glade within a fawning compass

Doom as a symptom of barren sunlight

Perch as a practice of alighting a stare

41.

A gaze comes undone at your touch. Where else may you turn an aside into a fallen clasp—as if you had understood fastening? Practice not standing in your own presence. When cemented to centuries of pretend fixations—which thoughts are real, and which bend to your weight? Which sounds can you make to distinguish between beckoning and becoming?

42.

Flames held in the mouth consume the breath which was once your speech. Stand in a corner while another fills two-dimensional air with toxins. The fourth dimension dims everything that is said so one can concentrate on the absent corona. When others' words leak with declarative glare practice releasing the flames from your mouth. Not as necessary seizures. Not as common burning but as the equivalent transmuted into a harmless spectrum of hands.

43.

The hands are invisible, but they orchestrate your kitchen. They rid you of unwanted visitors, advice, ill-fitting customs and the ceaseless chatter of corpses who cover themselves with plasticine commas, cornerstone leverage. If only amid loss quiet could descend.

44.

You do not wish loss even upon a shadow. Nor beckon a future which encumbers the spine. When unkind memorabilia wakes with no remedy, release a voice once echoed, once drowned. Emptied of eclipse put on these battered ellipses. Practice decipherment light. As if preordained, a cognizant dress staggers out to applaud the parting of your lips.

45.

Practice the word in itself as object, whose cloaked weight is perched within a sentence. Behaves as at a table around which others, throaty, gather to wait. Utterance is the object of their display. You rarely see a word in this way. Even less often do you consider that each character within the word is informed—with pleasure or disdain—against its others. Practice what you will make of the microcosm. Whose straight dotted eyes and sinuous lines will you permit to press, to unveil, to borrow your sound? Sometimes we choose who is beside us and other times we practice pretend compliance or active dispelling.

46.

Practice hiding under the ogre's bed. Acute, Unnecessary Perilousness
Syndrome. Wear several frocks, coats, and dresses. Leave your fingers,
balms and sources at home. Practice what you dream. If nothing comes
imagine the weltering spectacle of seven ogre's daughters delighting
in their beds. If you are caught you will need to utter only invented
words: cete, cit, pret. Explain the difference between rage and rag.
Run. When you return home rip the cover from a book and use the
blue backing as your name. Tuck up your gown and touch nothing
or you shall vanish instantly and find yourself in a location of only
invented companions. If this occurs, practice the grandest lingual
wedding as you fall down insensible to speech. When you recover
look in every body of water until you recognize the crimson of one
vowel.

47.

Snow interior portraits of the hours as they pass

In one window wanes an owl

An inner vestibule sighs

All visible slips should be driven in chariots

Walking sticks may crawl

Tea with squirrel at invocation helm

Kneel with sleeping-drink

Dressing gown pardons

Silken ropes scrawl

Punctuate balconies with glassy sea

Three o'clock verbiage drowns in a sink of downy mice

The vision is so close I can warm your breath against my brow

Look up to borrow bones from white skies

Petition fallen to stone steps outside a cottage door

The final hour is a fountain of lions

48.

Soft pleated policies bleach resurrected time. Trees were made from cider; dough was made from air. Not any mind, but his previous mind, made of soft tissue, pink electrical impulse—lisps. Drowning matter with computational intent. This is just a stance, and yet your fingers turn pages lobed and blue. Our bones always accompany us, though we rarely speak of them.

49.

This is the mind seeing for the first time that you do not resemble your portrait. Another stone, another mansion made of light. In a careful corridor, leaf approximates fox. Just as if she had emerged from a red, read lake. Certain beauty could be brought out, but is ignored, sidelong. If she had been in a book, you would flock to her. In modern passages the sounds we create are not sealed in soft wax. Hear the drone which is a verb between language and gesture—which moves through the room, corporeal, the wave of a russet torch.

50.

Practice the quiet in any room as a center of rectitude. When someone rises from a bench you hear the creak of wood before a voice which follows a body. If you anticipate sound before it is heard you frame a yellow sun with green rays in every direction. Surrounding the rays is a wash of blue and fragrant white. Scent of what will be said is another center the room opens. Inside such latitude we sit or walk and when a voice does emerge it colors the air.

51.

It may rain soon. One does not know when to end a brook, an encounter or lament. But praise often stops short pulling back into knees, inhaling caution. A sapling arcs in invisible wind. Hold out your arms to practice sight beyond skin. Nothing will surround you with a texture as important as air, as ruined as clover or penny. Less loss in this sentence than the previous. Undress careful weather until we appear clothed. We aren't going anywhere ever again. We must live in this upstairs bedroom, looking out the window. Have you ever met such a crystalline lens?

52.

Practice applauding mist, or mold it into morning. If you forget where you have been take careful impressions of all premises. To impress air, lean heavily into the space your body occupies. How to do this without falling? Practice having a voice containing speeches which allow you to rise when you have promised to be still.

53.

Practice putting on his bowtie before the concert and embracing a child who appears to be any height at all. You begin with a delicate bundle. Eventually you rise to your knees. When it comes to standing on tiptoe you must assure yourself that the thick white unknowing in the air is made of the tresses of one or another future.

54.

Remind yourself to be anyone you choose. Practice sitting still and trusting the thicket to thin itself silently. You will not see the silvered hands which pass in front of your eyes and you will not hear the thoughts which once sequestered your sleep.

When thoughts tire of pleading they will walk urgently in a direction away from your body. Animation in all outward forms is required for their existence. You may once have thought of these beggars as company.

When you arrive inside your inhabited self your movements are more intricate and thus invisible to petitioners. You believed them to be opposing and yet when you open your eyes you realize they have been discharged from your consciousness by your own impatient volition. Any that remain standing may be deserving of a proper burial.

55.

If you spend a quiet fortress in tears it may be necessary to spurn stillness. Mount ebony strings and run until breath demands cessation of crying. If you are unable to represent yourself, even in imaginary terms, you may watch a palette of sylvan days removed from your body. Like a creature enchanted by a remote cottage, your hopes revolve around the unmet inhabitants within. *A small and almost imperceptible chink through which the eye could just penetrate.* Remind yourself to be anyone you choose.

56.

Practice holding your hand, apologizing to a whisper, a crease in paper, a partial figure in a drawing. What drifted from us, bodies once beloved, adorned, now soft coal—remote eyes—we could not accept. If it is cold inside your house it is not cold inside your body. We spoke as if wading through a barren field, a fireplace dark with ash, folding a blanket near the surface of the sea. Unlacing your garments as if this would permit access to that which animates winged instruments within.

57.

How close we are to any living being. I don't know what I am
practicing. I've lost the loom, utterance, original stamp. Practice your
hands placed on keyed ivory, mounted boxwood, earth—in order
to bring yourself. If wind instruments then why not water? Walk
between windowpanes. Practice remembering where you used to live
as a maple neck—an offshoot of now.

58.

I sat in silence and removed all of myself. When he called my name I was a long way under. Where? Practicing paperwhite hours. Eighty-five beats per second. Transparent sheathe-wings hidden by outer shell. To all appearances, to him calling my name and entering the room, nothing had changed. There is a place one can exist where the boisterousness of mind is not a lesion. Engraved brass body. French, anonymous rosewood. Someone has saved these instruments we call watermarks. Though wading through leaves somewhat erased, we are able to see beyond multiple smudge marks, hear the silence of colors as the sky changes inside our closed eyes.

59.

Practical concerns may lure you away from assembling yourself on a daily basis. Running through trees. Hearing one's breath in any endeavor alongside a train and the child who speaks grenadine sentences, sniffles, trips upon himself stumbling down stairs. And now three persons ask you at once. Your forehead has fallen to the floor. We must leave in two minutes or be late. Voices grow into beaded hot liquid. Serpents are lost. Practice now, you are also that animal breathing quietly on a wooden bench. Head slightly bowed. Practice seeing yourself fully assembled, completely here, not cloistered in a future or withheld in the past. Pull your legs close and say nothing. You think that you have never seen a person within the perfect trust of closing eyes in unison, an inhabitant of the breath.

60.

Is the mind a place? A collage series of patchwork dresses? Are there predispositions? Practice attentiveness, unbroken by patterning of startlingly white plumage outside the window. What is it to draw in, to pull one's fingers to the center of a glove, to recoil and choose one's influences as carefully as one arranges a leaf in coat pocket. I could hear her voice but she was yellow, fallen. Could it be I have put myself aside as so many garments? Not to wear the weight of oneself? What did she wish to tell me in a lavender bedroom, up tiny jeweled stairs, light casting crystals upon walls? This portrait abbreviates everything.

61.

Practice entering the world we all inhabit but do not discuss. A falling leaf slows and rises up. The woman hidden inside the trunk of a dark tree raises her arms and lowers her branches, shaking apprehensive winter from her veins. A fox looks into my eyes, falters in ivy, molts to any animal with mottled limbs. When I tried on my wedding ring, seeing my hand for a moment as very old, knowing.

62.

Your absence grows bright and weary. We went downtown to a place no longer existent. Skylines intact. Stop sending messages to gutters. We are settling in to remember what we never knew. How to behave when everything disappears? I desire an equally desperate text to dictate my whereabouts. Running through trees. Milestones of cloakflower.

63.

The portrait I wish to emulate can be found in the landing, in a glass box. The moment we fear and the moment we seek, a dress tied to a tree. A key dangles from a thread and falls across her profile. Why would you agree to bed any noun amid abandon? These words will ultimately flee. A body slips, tied. My arms are leaves falling to the middle of a river, borrowed from a body which has no care.

64.

Practice images of oneself frozen in various attitudes or tasks. We take them out to remember. We pull them up from a river and are able to recall. Practice what the mind is made of, junction box for voices imprinting, chimera of electrical impulses. Practice being a brown bag on top of a shelf. A gun in a house. Practice who you were, tired, sounded out, handed over, head inside fettering spool. Practice disposing of your practice: time wasted and ruined, wasted and ruined.

65.

Why practice carrying carcasses of the unsaid
The weighty other world you did not visit

Practice prescriptive patience on a ledge
Sitting inside the weight of light

Practice whose hand tried to be someone
Tell me apocryphal, can air be fractional?

Practice no longer residing among the made
Not lying down one's head amid imaginary companions

Except when you must

66.

Practice a refusal you could only hollow with tears. Admiration beyond the polite hemisphere. You walk electrically beside me in a library. Unspoken messages cannot be silenced. Practice not feeding the perishable or the unreal. Repairing counsel, console, policy, particle, partner. Practice what will never be realized for so many bodily reasons—coinciding with eyes. Waking to your words, predawn, before the frozen can recall any imperfection in your imagined form.

ACKNOWLEDGEMENTS

The author wishes to gratefully acknowledge the following publications where some of these poems first appeared or are forthcoming:

Encylopedia Volume 3 L-Z, Hambone, Handsome, OnandOnScreen, Talisman.net

LAYNIE BROWNE

Laynie Browne is the author of twelve collections of poetry
and two novels. Her most recent collections of poems include
Scorpyn Odes (Kore Press 2015) and *Lost Parkour Ps(alms),* in two
editions, one in English, and another in French, from Presses
universitaires de Rouen et du Havré (2014). Her work appears
in *The Norton Anthology of Postmodern American Poetry,* second
editon (2013) as well as in *Ecopoetry: A Contemporary American
Anthology* (Trinity University Press, 2013). Her honors include:
a 2014 Pew Fellowship, the National Poetry Series Award, the
Contemporary Poetry Series Award, and two Gertrude Stein
Awards for Innovative American Poetry. She is co-editor of *I'll
Drown My Book: Conceptual Writing by Women* (Les Figues Press,
2012) and is currently editing an anthology of original essays
on the Poet's Novel. She teaches at University of Pennsylvania
and at Swarthmore College.

SPLITLEVEL TITLES

Laynie Browne, *PRACTICE*
Martin Corless-Smith, *This Fatal Looking Glass*
Alan Gilbert, *The Treatment of Monuments*
Carla Harryman, *W–/M–*
Lucy Ives, *The Worldkillers*
Catherine Meng, *The Longest Total Solar Eclipse of the Century*
Jerome Rothenberg, *A Cruel Nirvana*
Maged Zaher, *If Reality Doesn't Work Out*

CPSIA information can be obtained at www.ICGtesting.com
Printed in the USA
BVOW05s1617120515

399799BV00002B/2/P

9 780985 811167